DRAW 50 BEASTIES

AND YUGGLIES AND TURNOVER UGLIES AND THINGS THAT GO BUMP IN THE NIGHT

ALSO BY LEE J. AMES

DRAW 50 BEASTIES

AND YUGGLIES AND TURNOVER UGLIES AND THINGS THAT GO BUMP IN THE NIGHT

LEE J. AMES

Doubleday

NEW YORK   LONDON   TORONTO   SYDNEY   AUCKLAND

Published by Doubleday, a division of
Bantam Doubleday Dell Publishing Group, Inc.,
666 Fifth Avenue, New York, New York 10103.

Doubleday and the portrayal of an anchor with a dolphin
are trademarks of Doubleday, a division of
Bantam Doubleday Dell Publishing Group, Inc.

Library of Congress Cataloging-in-Publication Data

Ames, Lee J.
    Draw 50 beasties and yugglies and turnover uglies and things that
go bump in the night/Lee J. Ames. — 1st ed.
        p.   cm.
    Summary: Provides step-by-step instructions for drawing monsters,
goons, and gruesome beasts.
    1. Drawing—Technique—Juvenile literature. 2. Monsters in art—
Juvenile literature. [1. Drawing—Technique. 2. Monsters in
art.] I. Title. II. Title: Draw fifty beasties and yugglies and
turnover uglies and things that go bump in the night.
NC825.M6A46 1988
743′.6—dc19   88-16143
                        CIP
                        AC

ISBN 0-385-24625-0
    0-385-24626-9 (lib. bdg.)

For my grandkids, Lauren, Hilary, and Mark.
For Murray and Moo's grandkids, Melanie and Gregory.
For Warren and Chris's kids, Bryan and Drew.

TO THE READER

Perhaps by now you have come across one of my "Draw 50" books, or perhaps this is the first one you've ever picked up. Either way, I hope to show you in this book how to draw a wide variety of creatures—some creepy, some slimy, and others just plain funny (I hope). Where did I come up with this idea, you may ask? Well, mostly from your suggestions. When I'm not working in my studio, I often travel around the country visiting schools and book fairs, talking to people like you to find out what subjects they like to draw best. I have learned that monsters and strange-looking characters are definitely a favorite.

At first glance, the drawings in this book may appear difficult. But if you take your time and carefully follow the step-by-step instructions for each illustration, you will be able to produce a satisfying finished drawing.

To begin, you will need only clean paper, a pencil with moderately soft lead (HB or No. 2), and a kneaded eraser (available at art supply stores). Select the illustration you want to draw, and then *very lightly and carefully*, sketch out step number one. Then, also very *lightly and carefully*, add step number two to step number one. These steps, which may look the easiest, are the most important. A mistake here can ruin your entire drawing at the end. And remember to watch not only the lines themselves, but the *spaces between the lines* to make sure that they are the same as for the drawing in the book. As you sketch out these first steps, it might be a good idea to hold your work up to a mirror. Sometimes the mirror shows that you've twisted the drawing off to one side without being aware of it.

In each drawing, the new step is shown darker than the previous one so that it can be clearly seen. But you should keep your own work very light. Here's where the kneaded eraser will come in handy; use it to lighten your work after each step.

When you have finished your picture, you may want to go over it with some India ink. Apply this with a fine brush or pen. When the ink has thoroughly dried, erase the entire drawing with the kneaded eraser. The erasing will not affect the India ink.

The most important thing to remember is that even if your first attempts are not as good as you would like them to be, you should not get discouraged. Like any other talent, whether it be performing gymnastic feats or playing the piano, drawing takes practice to do your best.

Though there are many ways to learn how to draw, the step-by-step method used in this book should start you off in the right direction.

TO THE PARENT
OR TEACHER

"Leslie can draw the best beastie I ever saw!" Such peer acclaim and encouragement generate incentive. Contemporary methods of art instruction (freedom of expression, experimentation, self-evaluation of competence and growth) provide a vigorous, fresh-air approach for which we must all be grateful.

New ideas need not, however, totally exclude the old. One such is the "follow me, step-by-step" approach. In my young learning days this method was so common, and frequently so exclusive, that the student became nothing more than a pantographic extension of the teacher. In those days it was excessively overworked.

This does not mean that the young hand is never to be guided. Rather, specific guiding is fundamental. Step-by-step guiding that produces satisfactory results is valuable even when the means of accomplishment are not fully understood by the student.

The novice with a musical instrument is frequently taught to play simple melodies as quickly as possible, well before he or she learns the most elemental scratchings at the surface of music theory. The resultant self-satisfaction, pride in accomplishment, can provide significant motivation. And all from mimicking an instructor's "Do-as-I-do..."

Mimicry is prerequisite for developing creativity. We learn the use of our tools by mimicry. Then we can use those tools for creativity. To this end I would offer the budding artist the opportunity to memorize or mimic (rote-like, if you wish) the making of "pictures"—"pictures" he has been anxious to be able to draw.

The use of this book should be available to anyone who *wants* to try another way of flapping his wings. Perhaps he or she will then get off the ground when a friend says, "Leslie can draw the best beastie I ever saw!"

LEE J. AMES

DRAW 50 BEASTIES

AND YUGGLIES AND TURNOVER UGLIES AND THINGS THAT GO BUMP IN THE NIGHT

GAR GOYLE

GAR BOY

REGGIE VEGEHEAD

BULLY BELLY BRUNO

SPUD THE CRUD

EYE GORE

REED DICK YEWLISS

BEA ZARRE

LLEWELLEN NELL EWELL

ELBURT TRUBLE

DUDLEY YELDUD

MARGARET TERAGRAM

HERZZ ELF

GNOME BURWUN

GNOME BURT 000

BORED ERPA TROLL

HARB ORPA TROLL

DEACON TROLL

DEMON SSDRIBBLE

DEMON STRAIGHT

DEMON EYE IKKILL

IMP EARIE AL

SOPHIE STICK CAT

TRA PICKLEFISH

MELON COLLIE

SARA TRITOPS

DIPPY LODDACUSS

TERRY ANNA DUNN

TYRONE IZ SORUS

DRIBBLE PUSS

SLIMY SLOPKISSER

AWESOME MINOTAUR

LOONY PUNYCORN

MIKE THE VIKE

DIZZ TRAWYER

BLACK HOLE DEGRUJJ

KHAZ MCDUST

MINI MOOM

LEE J. AMES joined the Doubleday list in 1962, and since that time his popular drawing books have sold close to one and a half million copies. Utilizing a unique, step-by-step method to guide the young artist's hand, Ames's "Draw 50" books have inspired the creativity of countless children (and adults).

His artistic experience runs the gamut from working at Walt Disney Studios in the days when *Fantasia* and *Pinocchio* were created to teaching at New York City's School of Visual Arts to running his own advertising agency. In addition, he has illustrated over 150 books, from preschool picture books to postgraduate texts.

When not working in his studio, Lee can be found on the tennis courts in Long Island, New York, where he currently lives with his wife, Jocelyn.